WORLD RELIGIONS

SIKHISM

Kanwaljit Kaur-Singh

Thomson Learning
New York

Words appearing in *italic* in the text have not fallen into common English usage. The publishers have followed Merriam Webster's Collegiate Dictionary (Tenth Edition) for spelling and usage.

First published in the United States in 1995 by
Thomson Learning
New York, NY

Published simultaneously in Great Britain by Wayland (Publishers) Ltd.

U.S. copyright © 1995 Thomson Learning

U.K. copyright © 1995 Wayland Publishers Ltd.

Library of Congress Cataloging-in-Publication Data
Kaur-Singh, Kanwaljit.
  Sikhism / Kanwaljit Kaur-Singh.
        p.   cm.—(World religions)
  Includes bibliographical references and index.
  ISBN 1-56847-379-6 (hardcover)
  1. Sikhism—Juvenile literature. I. Title. II. Series.
  BL2018.K28   1995
  294.6—dc20   95–4711

Printed in Italy

Cover: A Sikh couple outside their home.
Title page: Sikhs walking through the main gateway to go into the Golden Temple.
Contents page: The Harimandir Sahib, more commonly known as the Golden Temple, in Amritsar.

Acknowledgments

The author thanks Indarjit Singh, editor of the *Sikh Messenger*, for his help and advice.
The author and publishers thank the following for their permission to reproduce photographs: Circa Photo Library: *cover*, 5 (bottom), 24, 29, 31 (bottom); Guy Hall, 34 (top); Christine Osborne: 21, 25, 26, 27, 30, 31 (top), 33, 34 (bottom), 36, 38, 43; TRIP: *title page*, 3, 4, 5 (top), 6, 7, 8, 10, 11, 12, 14, 15, 16, 17, 18, 20, 44 (H. Rogers); 23 (P. J. Hicks); 42, 45 (B. Dhanjul). The photographs on pages 19, 32, and 35 were taken by the author.

Contents

INTRODUCTION

GURUS

In Indian languages the word *guru* means "teacher." Sikhs use the word only for the founder of their religion, Guru Nanak, his nine successors, and the Guru Granth Sahib, the Sikh book of scriptures. For Sikhs, a guru is a spiritual guide who teaches God's message to humanity.

Guru Nanak started Sikhism in the fifteenth century in the Punjab area of northern India. Today this is still where the majority of Sikhs live, but there are also many in other countries around the world. Male Sikhs are easily recognized by their turbans and beards. Sikh females have uncut hair, left loose or tied neatly in a bun at the back of the head.

The basic and most important beliefs and ideas of Sikhism are as follows:

- There is only one God.
- All human beings are equal.
- All religions should be accepted.
- Men and women are equal.
- It is good to serve others.

Guru Nanak and the nine gurus who followed him all taught these ideas, and practiced the teachings to show their importance in daily life.

Sikhs believe in one God who is neither male nor female, but is imageless, formless; who is not born and never dies; and who is present everywhere in the universe. They believe God the creator made one humanity, that no person is high or low by birth, and that it is actions that make people good or evil. The idea that all humans are equal is fundamental to Sikhism.

Sikhs think that different religions are different paths leading to God, and that no single religion is the only true one. They respect other people's beliefs. For

Young Sikh people at the gurdwara

Sikhs, showing respect for other faiths goes as far as laying down one's own life for the sake of others. Guru Tegh Bahadur, the ninth guru, did this. He was executed for defending the rights of Hindus to follow their religion.

Guru Nanak chose who would follow him as the next guru, and each guru chose his successor in the same way. Guru Gobind Singh, the tenth guru, did not pass the guruship to a person, but to the Sikh scriptures. This is why the Sikh book of scriptures is called the Guru Granth Sahib. It contains the writings of the Sikh gurus and also of followers of other faiths.

Sikhs believe that the highest authority is God, and that God's truth is revealed through the Guru Granth Sahib. Because the Guru Granth Sahib takes the place of the living guru, it is treated with the utmost respect. It is central to Sikh daily practices, ceremonies, and festivals.

Anyone can come to pray at the Sikh place of worship, called the *gurdwara*. Regardless of their social status, all worshipers sit on the floor. There are no places or areas kept especially for certain people. Men and women are given equal positions, and both take part in leading services and conducting ceremonies.

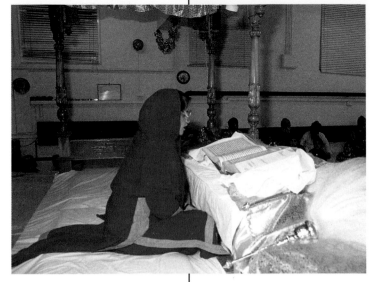

A Sikh woman reading the Guru Granth Sahib in the gurdwara

Preparing langar *in the* gurdwara

At home in Amritsar. Nearly every Sikh family has a picture of the Golden Temple at home.

Each gurdwara contains a *langar*, or common kitchen, and after every service all the members of the congregation eat together. This puts into practice the idea that everyone is equal. Men and women from the congregation, of all classes and colors, prepare and serve the food.

One of the most important and best-known gurdwaras is the Golden Temple in Amritsar, India. It was built during the time of the fifth Guru, Arjan Dev, in 1588. When the building was finished, the Guru installed the Guru Granth Sahib there. In 1803, the Sikh Maharaja (prince) Ranjit Singh covered the top half of the building with gold leaf, and so the *gurdwara* got its present name.

There are three principles on which Sikhs try to base their lives:

- *Nam Japna* – remembering God
- *Kirat Karni* – earning a living by honest means and hard work
- *Vand Chhakna* – sharing with people who are less fortunate than themselves.

As an example of sharing and serving, Sikhs remember the story of Bhai Kanahya. During a battle between the Mogul emperor's forces and Sikhs, Bhai Kanahya was providing drinking water to the wounded. Some Sikh soldiers complained that he was giving water to the enemy's soldiers. He was charged with helping the enemy and brought before Guru Gobind Singh, the tenth guru. He explained to the Guru, "I do not see a friend or a foe, but only human beings." The Guru was pleased with this and blessed Bhai Kanahya for his true Sikh spirit of service.

1

THE STORY OF SIKHISM

Guru Nanak

Guru Nanak, the founder of Sikhism, was born in 1469 C.E. (Common Era; see page 47), at Talwandi in north India. Since then, the town has been renamed Nanakana Sahib, and it is now in Pakistan. Nanak was born a Hindu. His father was Mehta Kalu, his mother was Tripta, and he had a sister named Nanaki. As a young boy, Nanak showed great interest in listening and learning about God and people. He worked as a cattle herder and then as an accountant, and spent a large amount of his wages on feeding the hungry and poor.

A painting of Guru Nanak, who started to think about God as he was tending cattle.

From an early age Nanak was unhappy about the religious practices around him. There is a story of how he received God's message when he was 30 years old.

At the time that Guru Nanak was born, Indian society was suffering political, social, and religious disputes. People called the Moguls were invading India from the north. Most people in India were followers of the Hindu religion. The Moguls were Muslims and were determined to convert Hindus to Islam.

7

One morning, he went to bathe in the river. He disappeared for some days and people thought he must have drowned.

Three days later he reappeared but remained silent for one day. Then he announced: "There is neither Hindu nor Muslim, only God's path. I shall follow God's path." He explained that he had been taken to God and been blessed. God had asked Nanak to rejoice in God's name and to teach others to do so.

Guru Nanak made four long journeys to spread his message about God's truth and the way to lead a truthful life. He taught that all human beings, black or white, rich or poor, high or low, men or women, are equal in God's eyes. He said that God is not interested in religious labels. What matters is the way people behave.

The guru taught that women are equal to men, and wrote "How can we call her bad, who gives birth to great people?"

A succession of gurus

Guru Nanak believed that it was important to teach by example. He said: "Truth is high, but higher still is truthful living." He decided to start a succession of Gurus, who would practice the teachings. He appointed Guru Angad Dev to be the guru after him, and each guru after that chose the next one.

An artist's impression of the ten gurus and the Guru Granth Sahib. Guru Nanak is at the top center, the second to the fifth gurus are on the left, the sixth to the ninth gurus are on the right, and Guru Gobind Singh, the tenth guru, is bottom center.

THE TEN HUMAN GURUS

1499-1539 Guru Nanak, the first guru – Founded Sikhism.

1539-52 Guru Angad Dev, the second guru –
Improved the Gurmukhi script for writing Panjabi, which was the language of ordinary people in the Punjab. All the gurus wrote in Panjabi, so the scriptures became available to everyone. Guru Angad Dev also encouraged sports.

1552-74 Guru Amar Das, the third guru –
Organized the growing number of Sikhs into groups and established centers, with men and women as leaders, for spreading the guru's message. He opposed the caste system, which divided Indian society, by encouraging all people to sit together to eat in the *langar*.

1574-81 Guru Ram Das, the fourth guru –
Founded the city of Amritsar and encouraged tradesmen to settle there. It soon grew into a great trading and religious center. Guru Ram Das also composed many *shabads* (hymns), including *Lavan*, which is the central part of the Sikh marriage ceremony.

1581-1606 Guru Arjan Dev, the fifth guru –
Built the Harimandir Sahib, which is now known as the Golden Temple. He also collected the writings of the first four Gurus, his own, and those of many Hindu and Muslim holy people, and compiled them into the Adi Granth, more commonly known as the Guru Granth Sahib. The Mogul emperor Jehangir tried to force the guru to become a Muslim and also to make changes to the Guru Granth Sahib. When the guru refused, he was tortured to death.

1606-44 Guru Hargobind, the sixth guru –
Wore two swords, one symbolizing the spiritual power of God's truth and the other showing his readiness to use actual physical power to defend the weak and the helpless. His claim to have both spiritual and physical power brought the guru into conflict with Jehangir, who imprisoned him. When the guru was released, he refused to go unless 52 rajas (princes) were also set free. In the end, the 52 rajas were allowed to leave the prison holding the guru's cloak (see page 44).

THE TEN HUMAN GURUS

1644-61 Guru Har Rai, the seventh guru –
Opened free hospitals and dispensaries offering medical services to the sick and the needy.

1661-64 Guru Harkrishan, the eighth guru –
Continued serving the sick during a smallpox epidemic in Delhi. He caught the disease and died at the age of eight.

1664-75 Guru Tegh Bahadur, the ninth guru –
Traveled far and wide to preach God's message. He was executed by the Mogul emperor Aurangzeb for his belief in the basic human right of people to worship as they choose.

1675-1708 Guru Gobind Singh, the tenth and the last human guru –
Created the Khalsa (see page 12) and fought many battles to defend his community. His two older sons died in battle, and the younger two were walled up alive for refusing to accept Islam. Guru Gobind Singh passed the guruship on to the Guru Granth Sahib, so ending the line of human gurus.

Note: The dates given are for the guruship of each guru.

Baba Buddha used to sit under this tree while supervising the building of the Golden Temple. Baba Buddha was a highly respected Sikh who had met Guru Nanak when he was only nine and who performed the rite of bestowing the title of guru to the second, third, fourth, fifth, and sixth gurus.

The Mogul empire

In 1526 the Moguls conquered northern India and established their empire, with its base in Delhi. They continued to expand the empire throughout the sixteenth and seventeenth centuries. The first emperors including Akbar (1556-1605) allowed followers of different religions to worship as they wished. However, the emperors who came after Akbar, such as Jehangir (1605-27) and Aurangzeb (1658-1707), were determined that all the people living in the empire should convert to Islam. Hindus and Sikhs were persecuted, and many were killed for refusing to give up their religion. Guru Arjan Dev, the fifth guru, and Guru Tegh Bahadur, the ninth guru, were both put to death for standing up for religious freedom.

The Gurdwara Bangla Sahib in Delhi was built on the spot where Guru Harkrishan, the eighth Guru, cared for victims of smallpox and died from the disease himself.

THE MARTYRDOM OF GURU TEGH BAHADUR

The Sikh gurus taught that it is a fundamental duty of every human being to respect the religious beliefs of others. Guru Tegh Bahadur, the ninth guru, set an example for this by laying down his life to uphold the rights of Hindu believers. At this time, the Mogul emperor Aurangzeb (1658-1707) was forcing Hindus and Sikhs to accept Islam, and killing many of those who refused. Some Brahmans (members of the Hindu priestly class) from Kashmir asked Guru Tegh Bahadur for help.

The guru believed that all people had the right to worship as they wished, and so he agreed to speak to Aurangzeb on the Brahmans' behalf. He told the Brahmans to tell the emperor that, if the the emperor could persuade the guru to accept Islam, the Hindu community would also accept Islam. The guru was called to the emperor in Delhi. He was not persuaded to renounce his beliefs, despite bribery and threats, and was beheaded.

11

THE CREATION OF THE KHALSA

Following the martyrdom of Guru Tegh Bahadur, Guru Gobind Singh decided to organize the Sikh community so that Sikhs would be able to defend themselves.

In 1699, crowds of Sikhs gathered in Anandpur for their new year festival, *Baisakhi*. The guru welcomed them and praised them for their devotion. Then he drew his sword and asked for the head of a Sikh who was prepared to give his life for the faith. There was silence. At the guru's third call, a Sikh stepped forward and offered his head. The guru took him into a nearby tent and then returned, his sword dripping with blood. He repeated his demand four more times, and four more men offered themselves. The congregation saw each man being taken into the tent. After some time, the guru appeared again, with all five men still alive. The guru explained that this had been a test of their courage and willingness to die for their faith and the guru. The Sikh community had passed the test.

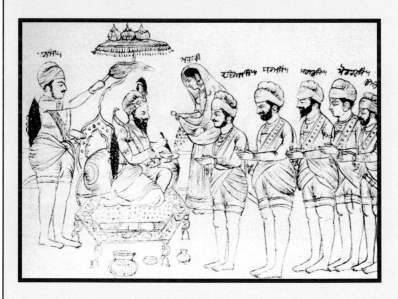

The Panj Piarey *are ready to receive* amrit. *As Guru Gobind Singh's wife, Mata Sundri, gives him sugar crystals, he says "Your contribution has made the ceremony complete."*

He called the five men *Panj Piarey* (Five Beloved Ones) and performed a ceremony called *amrit* to initiate them into the *Khalsa*, the Sikh community. Thousands more men and women also took *amrit* and joined the *Khalsa* on that day. The men were given the title *singh* (lion) and the women were given the name *kaur* (princess). The Guru told them all to wear the five ks as symbols of their faith. This uniform would identify them. Even in moments of weakness, they could not then deny their faith.

The Mogul empire disintegrated during the eighteenth century. Toward the end of Mogul rule in the Punjab, the emperors offered rewards to anyone who could bring them the head or any part of a Sikh's body. Sikhs left their homes and hid in the jungles for safety, refusing to abandon their faith even in the face of torture and death. This period, from 1708 to 1739, was the worst suffering in Sikh history.

Sikhs as rulers

From 1739, foreign armies invaded India on many occasions. Sikhs fought and defeated the invaders at the northwest frontier and they eventually established their own independent states in this area. Twelve of the states became powerful and were known as the *Misals*.

Maharaja Ranjit Singh was the ruler of one of the Sikh states. He fought the other Sikh chiefs, to unite all the states, and went on to defeat other rulers and to declare himself emperor of a huge area of India in 1799. He treated people of all religions equally. Muslims, Hindus, and Sikhs filled important posts in his empire.

After the death of Maharaja Ranjit Singh in 1839, feuding among different parts of the Sikh empire led to its collapse within ten years. The British took the opportunity of annexing the large northern Indian province of Punjab. They deposed the 12-year-old Maharaja Dalip Singh and made him present the famous Koh-i-noor diamond, which Maharaja Ranjit Singh had received from an Afghan prince, to Queen Victoria. The Maharaja was ordered to live in England, where he died in 1893.

British rule, 1858-1947

The British respected the Sikhs for their bravery and encouraged them to join the British army. However, the Sikhs became unhappy with the British government of India, the Raj, as the British allowed the historic *gurdwaras* to fall into the hands of non-Sikhs.

THE FIVE Ks

The five ks can be called the uniform of Sikhs. They are worn by men and women.

Kes – uncut hair. Men tie their hair on top of their heads and cover it with turbans.

Kanga – a small wooden comb, worn to keep the hair neat. It represents cleanliness.

Kara – a steel or iron bangle. It is not worn as jewelry, but as a symbol reminding Sikhs of their duty to do right.

Kachh – undershorts. They are a symbol reminding Sikhs of their vow of sexual purity and self-control.

Kirpan – a sword. This is a symbol of God's supreme power and also reminds Sikhs of their duty to defend the weak.

The Sikhs started to protest peacefully for the right to manage their *gurdwaras*, and this was finally granted to them, after twenty years, in 1925.

Sikhs in independent India

India gained its independence in 1947. The state of Punjab, where most Sikhs lived, was divided, one third becoming part of India and the rest becoming part of what is now Pakistan. At that point, many Sikhs went to live in other parts of the world.

Rebuilding the Akal Takhat after it had been destroyed during the attack on the Golden Temple in 1984

From the beginning, the Sikhs in India felt that the Indian government and the Hindu majority (about 83 percent) treated them unfairly. Sikh leaders started a protest campaign to try to get their grievances resolved. In 1984, in response to Sikh unrest, the Prime Minister of India at that time, Indira Gandhi, ordered an attack on the Golden Temple and all the other Sikh historic *gurdwaras*. The attack took place on the day Sikhs were commemorating the martyrdom of Guru Arjan Dev. The government said that the reason for the attack was that there were Sikh terrorists hiding in the Golden Temple. No explanation was given for the attacks on 36 other *gurdwaras* that happened at the same time.

During the attack, thousands of Sikhs were killed. The Golden Temple and the Guru Granth Sahib were badly damaged. The Sikh reference library, containing manuscripts and original writings of the Gurus, was destroyed. Priceless jewels were looted, other artifacts were burned, and the Akal Takhat, one of the most important holy places in the Golden Temple precincts, was almost demolished. The attack and the following torture of Sikhs deeply outraged the whole Sikh world.

Since then the gulf between Sikhs and the Indian government has widened, and many Sikhs are campaigning to establish their own independent state.

A Sikh farmer in the Punjab

SIKH GRIEVANCES

The following are some of the grievances of Sikhs since Indian independence:

Punjab is one of 16 Indian states. Each state was given the right to have its own official language, but in practice it took 20 years of protest, during which thousands of Sikhs were jailed, for the state of Punjab to receive this right. Sikhs still do not have an independent identity in the Indian constitution; all are referred to as Hindus.

The capital of Punjab, Chandigarh, has still not been given to Punjab, in spite of many promises. The city has the status of a union territory, which means that it is directly controlled by the central government.

Punjab is sometimes called the "breadbasket" of India, since it produces three-quarters of the country's total wheat. The central government pays Punjabi farmers, who are mostly Sikhs, less for their wheat than it pays farmers in other states.

Similarly, electricity generated in Punjab is sold more cheaply to neighboring states than to Punjab, and these states are also allowed more power than the Punjab itself. As a result, the Sikhs in Punjab have to work harder, and at inconvenient hours, to use power to irrigate their land.

A carpenter in Amritsar, with pictures of the gurus in his box

2

THE WORLD OF SIKHS

Sikhs in India

Sikhism began in the Punjab area of northern India. Today Punjab is one of the 16 states of India. It is sometimes called the "homeland of Sikhs," because the majority of Sikhs in the world (approximately 14 million) still live there. Their language is Panjabi. The Panjabi word *punj* means "five" and *ab* means "water," so *Punjab* is the "land of five rivers." The river waters make the land fertile, and most Sikhs in the Punjab are farmers.

In 1947, when India became independent, the land of the Punjab was divided. One third of it remained part of India, as the state of Punjab. The rest became part of a separate Muslim state called West Pakistan. Over two million Sikhs left their homes and lands in West Pakistan. They could not all settle in the Punjab, and many went to other Indian states such as Haryana, Uttar Pradesh, Maharashtra, and Jammu and Kashmir. Sikhs today are two percent of the total population of India.

Some 60 percent of Sikhs in India live in the state of Punjab and 20 percent in Chandigarh.

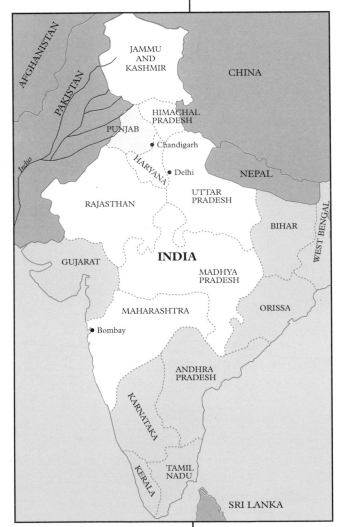

Sikhs throughout the world

At the beginning of the twentieth century, the British ruled India and East Africa. They took skilled Indians including Sikhs from the Punjab to help build railroads in East Africa, and so Sikhs came to live in what are now Kenya, Uganda, and Tanzania. They achieved success in various businesses and professions and became prosperous.

When the East African countries became independent, beginning in the 1960s, Sikhs living there faced many difficulties. The military dictators and other rulers did not want the Indians to continue enjoying their prosperity. In 1972, General Idi Amin, the President of Uganda at that time, actually forced all Indians including Sikhs to leave the country. Most of the Sikhs in Africa had British passports, and so, in the unsettled atmosphere of the 1960s and 1970s, many of them moved to Great Britain. Large numbers also went to Canada and the United States.

More recently, the Ugandan government has invited the Indians back to the country and has returned all lands and other properties that had been taken from them. Today Sikhs are respected in East African countries and their language, Panjabi, has the status of one of the main languages there.

A street in Amritsar. This city has always been a center of the Sikh religion.

17

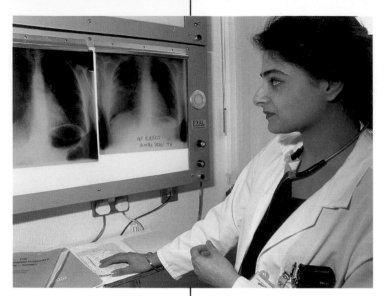

At the end of the twentieth century, Sikhs live worldwide. Some have made their homes in Australia, Southeast Asia (including Singapore and Malaysia), Africa, the United States, Canada, Great Britain, and some other European countries. In Western countries Sikhs have sometimes suffered because of the racist attitudes of the host communities.

Many Sikhs in the West work as doctors

Sikhs in Great Britain

There are about 400,000 Sikhs in Great Britain, most of whom live in large cities. They have come mainly from India and East Africa. Wherever Sikhs have settled, they have collected money to buy either land, where they can build a *gurdwara*, or an old building, which they can turn into a *gurdwara*. There are more than 200 gurdwaras in Great Britain now.

After the partition of Punjab in 1947, many Sikhs lost their land. They could find no employment in India, but there were job opportunities in Great Britain; and as members of the British Commonwealth, Indians including Sikhs were free to move to Great Britain. When they arrived, they faced many difficulties. Some British people do not try to understand why Sikh men wear turbans, and young boys are teased because their hair is in braids or they wear a *patka* (small turban). Sometimes Sikhs have been refused jobs because they wear turbans, or their employers have insisted that they cut their hair or wear helmets or caps. One school would not allow a Sikh boy to attend wearing a turban. But tolerance has generally prevailed. Prejudice in some areas has often been balanced by sympathetic understanding. For example, British law requiring all motorcycle riders to wear helmets was amended to exempt Sikhs.

Sikhs in Great Britain have made some changes in their religious practices. Since Sunday is a public holiday, it is a convenient day for Sikhs to attend the *gurdwara*. The celebration of a festival, even if it falls during the week, is moved to the weekend. Religious processions, which are an important part of festivals in the Punjab, are not common in Great Britain. Perhaps because of the poor weather, Sikhs in Great Britain often use *gurdwaras* for weddings and death ceremonies, whereas in India they would hold these in the open air. There have been some social changes, too. Sometimes the extended family system breaks down, and divorce, rarely heard of among Sikhs, is becoming more common.

Sikhs in North America

There are about 250,000 practicing Sikhs of Indian origin in the United States and another 200,000 in Canada. In the United States, Sikhs settled first in Stockton, El Centro, and Yuba City in California. Now there are also large numbers of Sikhs also in other big cities such as Washington and New York, but the main Sikh communities live are on the West Coast. There are about 90 *gurdwaras* scattered all over the United States.

Sikhs went to Canada in the early 1960s, when anyone who found a job there was allowed to stay. In the 1970s Canadian policy changed and people had to obtain entry permits before they could move there. Sikhs in Canada live mainly in Vancouver, Ottawa, Edmonton, Montreal, Toronto, and Calgary. They have important positions in all types of businesses and professions. There are about 125 *gurdwaras* in Canada.

3HO

Sikhism in the United States is being influenced by a steadily growing movement known as 3HO, the Healthy, Happy, and Holy Organization. This was started by Harbhajan Singh, known as Yogi Bhajan. In 1969, some Americans converted to Sikhism through contact with this organization. They were given *amrit*. There have been other conversions since.

Sikhs took part in a multifaith procession during a meeting of world religions in Chicago.

3

GURBANI

The writings in the Guru Granth Sahib are called Gurbani, meaning the "word of the Guru."

The Guru Granth Sahib is written in the Panjabi language, and the script used is Gurmukhi. All copies of the Guru Granth Sahib are exactly the same and have 1430 pages. They may be printed only by the Shiromani Gurdwara Parbandhak Committee, the governing body of the Sikh *gurdwaras* of Punjab. There are English translations to help understanding, but they are never used in place of the original Panjabi version.

THE GURU GRANTH SAHIB

Sikhs believe that God's truth is revealed through the teachings of the Sikh gurus, which are contained in the Guru Granth Sahib.

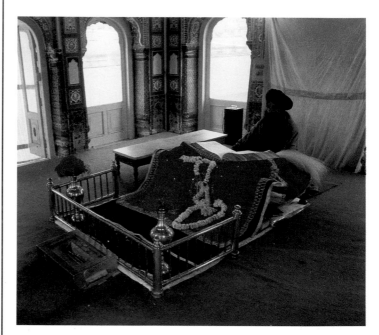

The Guru Granth Sahib, the Sikh book of scriptures, in an upper room of the Golden Temple

Guru Arjan Dev, the fifth guru, collected together all the writings of the first four gurus. To these he added his own writings and those of Hindu and Muslim holy people, whose views were in accord with Sikh teachings, to make the Adi Granth. The word *Adi* means "first" (both in time and in importance) and *Granth* means "collection." Later on, Guru Gobind Singh, the tenth guru, added the writings of Guru Tegh Bahadur and decreed that Sikhs should follow the Adi Granth as their next guru. Therefore the Adi Granth became known as the Guru Granth Sahib.

THE MOOL MANTRA

The Guru Granth Sahib begins with the Mool Mantra, which contains Guru Nanak's description of God:

> There is one and only one God
> Whose name is Truth.
> God the creator is without fear, without hate, immortal,
> Without form and is beyond birth and death
> And is understood through God's grace.
>
> (Guru Granth Sahib, p. 1)

This sets out the Sikh belief that there is only one God, who is the creator of all humanity. One can understand God by acting upon the gurus' teachings. God's acceptance of the sincerity of our actions is called his grace. In the Gurmukhi script, the Mool Mantra opens with ੴ, meaning One God.

Respect for the Guru Granth Sahib

The Guru Granth Sahib takes the place of the living gurus among Sikhs, and so they treat it with great respect and the kind of reverence that would have been shown to the ten human gurus. Sikhs do not worship the Guru Granth Sahib, but revere the "word" revealed through its *shabads* (hymns).

Every morning in a *gurdwara*, the Guru Granth Sahib is brought from the small room where it is kept overnight and installed ceremoniously on a platform (the *palki*) with a canopy (*chandni*) above it. It rests on cushions and is covered with a cloth (*romallas*). A member of the *sangat* (congregation) remains in constant attendance and waves a *chouri* (fan) over the book, as a sign of its sovereignty.

A Sikh waving the chouri *as he reads the Guru Granth Sahib*

AKHAND PATH

On festivals and special family occasions, a chain of people read out the entire Guru Granth Sahib, from beginning to end. This continuous reading is called *Akhand Path*. It usually takes about 48 hours.

EQUALITY

The following *shabad* expresses the Sikh idea that all human beings are equal:

> God first created Light.
> From the Lord's play all living creatures came
> And from the Divine Light the whole creation
>   sprang.
> Why then should we divide human creatures
> Into the high and the low?
>
> Friend, be not in error:
> Out of the Creator creation comes.
> Everywhere in creation the Creator is.
> The Lord's Spirit is all pervading!
>
> The Lord, the Maker, has molded one mass of
>   clay
> Into vessels of diverse shapes.
> Free from taint are all the vessels of clay
> Since free from taint is the Divine Potter.
>
> The True One pervades all things.
> All things come to pass as the Lord ordains.
> He who has understood the Divine Will
> Recognizes only the One Reality—
> And he alone is what a person ought to be.

(Guru Granth Sahib, p. 1349)

God ("the Divine Potter") creates all humans from the same material ("clay"). They may all be different ("vessels of diverse shapes"), but they are all without fault ("free from taint"). Therefore it is wrong to judge that some people are better or worse than others.

Everything that happens is according to God's will ("as the Lord ordains"). Anyone who understands this is a true follower of God.

Worshipers enter the presence of the Guru Granth Sahib without shoes and with their heads covered. They bow and touch their foreheads on the floor before sitting down. These are all marks of respect.

Any man or woman may read the Guru Granth Sahib to the congregation, but quite often it is read by an appointed *granthi* (reader), who performs ceremonies and leads prayers. After evening prayers, the Guru Granth Sahib is ceremoniously closed and put away again in its own small room.

Ragees *performing* kirtan *in Kampala, Uganda*

Other Sikh writings

The Guru Granth Sahib contains the teachings of the first nine gurus, but does not give all the teachings of Guru Gobind Singh, the tenth guru, and does not record the final phase of the development of the Sikh community. For these things, Sikhs turn to several other books.

The Dasam Granth includes the writings of Guru Gobind Singh and of 52 poets, who were in the guru's service. Bhai Gurdas Dian Vara is a source of information about the lives and teachings of the first five gurus, and the Hukamnamas are letters written by the gurus to their followers. Sikhs who lived at the same time as Guru Gobind Singh wrote the Rehatnamas to explain the Sikh code of conduct. In 1945, the Shiromani Gurdwara Parbandhak Committee compiled the Rehat Maryada, which is a guide to the Sikh way of life.

SHABADS

The entire Guru Granth Sahib is written in poetry, arranged in stanzas (groups of lines) called *shabads*. The *shabads* can be sung, and many *gurdwaras* employ professional singers called *ragees* to sing the *shabads* during services. Singing of the *shabads* is called *kirtan*.

4

HOME AND FAMILY LIFE

During the time of Guru Nanak, many people in India thought highly of yogis, men who cut themselves off from normal worldly activities and adopted a life of poverty and meditation in the belief that this was a way for their spirit to be reunited with God. These men left their families and other ordinary human contacts. Guru Nanak pointed out that they nonetheless needed the help of people who did live in ordinary families:

> For food and clothes, these holy men still go from door to door begging.   (GGS, p. 879)

Sikh children praying at home

Sikhs do not believe that it is necessary to withdraw from normal life to find God.

The guru writes:

> Living within the family one finds God.
> (GGS, p. 661)

All the gurus except Guru Harkrishan, who died at the age of eight, were married and had children, and they encouraged their followers to marry.

Extended families

It is still common among Sikhs today for different generations and branches of a family all to live together. This traditional extended family system has its roots in Sikh teachings that different age groups should show one another respect and feel responsible for one another. In close-knit families, children accompany their parents when they visit friends and relatives, go to the *gurdwara*, and attend formal and informal events.

It is becoming more difficult for people to live in extended families today, however. People have to move away from home in search of employment. Also, in Great Britain for example, Sikhs cannot find affordable accommodations to house their whole extended families. It is common therefore for grandparents, uncles and aunts, and brothers and sisters to live in separate houses, but all close to one another.

When Sikhs go to the gurdwara, they give money for charity before they bow down to the Guru Granth Sahib.

Marriage

Sikhism emphasizes the importance of marriage and teaches that, in a marriage, the man and woman are equal partners. The Sikh gurus said that marriage is not only a civil or social contract, but also a spiritual union between two equal partners in which they support each other and enrich each other's lives.

Also, a marriage does not remain a private matter between two persons. Through the couple, two families become closely connected. Therefore, family and friends assist in finding suitable partners, although the couple themselves decide whether to marry. Sikh marriages of this kind are better described as assisted marriages rather than as arranged ones.

Sikhism gives guidance on responsibilities in marriage. The couple should try to make their union perfect and happy on all levels; physical, material, intellectual, emotional, and spiritual. The husband and wife should stay absolutely faithful to one another and treat their marriage as permanent. In this way, they help ensure that the value of marriage is understood by other people in the future. However, the Sikh religion and tradition do not rule out the possibility of divorce if a marriage breaks down completely.

Parents and children

The older members of a family teach the children about Sikh history and the Sikh way of life and try to show them the importance of love and respect and of being prepared to give up what they want for themselves in order to help others. Children go to the *gurdwara* with their families and learn to cook and serve meals in the *langar*.

The mother puts a garland on the groom after the wedding service

The gurus' teachings tell parents that their children are gifts that God entrusts to them. It is therefore the parents' duty to give their best to their children in all aspects of life, including religion. Sikh parents must show their children the principles of Sikhism, and, when fulfilling their obligations toward their children, they must not expect anything in return.

The Guru Granth Sahib has teachings for children, too. They should respect their elders and look after them when they are old and weak, as they cared for the children when they were young and helpless. The guru says:

> Son, why do you quarrel with your father ? Due to him you have grown to this age.   (GGS, p. 1200)

Two Sikh boys (center and right) serving langar *with a Hindu friend*

Worship in the home

Worship is a part of daily life at home. After their morning wash, Sikhs start the day by meditating on God and His attributes. There is no special posture in which Sikhs meditate. Young children are encouraged to repeat the name *Waheguru* (wonderful Lord).

CLOTHES

Sikhs wear either Western or traditional clothes.

Men mostly wear Western-style trousers and jackets. Sometimes men wear the traditional *kurta* (a long, loose shirt) and jodhpur-style trousers.

Women mostly wear Punjabi suits, which consist of *kameez* (dress), *salwar* (trousers), and *dupatta* (scarf). These clothes are usually made of brightly colored cottons, silks, and chiffons. Clothes for special occasions are embroidered with silk, silver, or gold threads.

Instead of full turbans, young boys sometimes wear small turbans called *patkas* or they braid their uncut hair and tie it at the back of the neck or on top of the head.

Sikhs use set passages from the Guru Granth Sahib for morning prayers. If time is short, they can recite these passages while getting ready for their day's work and going about their usual activities. There are also set passages for evening and bedtime prayers.

Some Sikh families set aside a room of their home where the Guru Granth Sahib is kept. They call this room their *gurdwara*, and they may all join there for prayer in the mornings and evenings. Sometimes friends and relatives come, too.

Sikh worship can take place anywhere. It involves very little ritual, so no priests are needed to lead the worship. Any Sikh man or woman may conduct ceremonies, sing hymns, or speak about the religion in the presence of the Guru Granth Sahib. In places in the world where there are not many Sikhs, there may be no *gurdwara* for them to attend. In such places, worship at home has a special importance.

5

COMMUNITY LIFE

The gurdwara

The name *gurdwara* for a Sikh place of worship literally means "the door of the Guru." Some of the historic *gurdwaras* in India are splendid buildings, but a *gurdwara* can be set up in any place where the Guru Granth Sahib is kept. Whatever the building is likc, a *gurdwara* has the Sikh flag, the *Nishan Sahib*, flying outside.

A *gurdwara* building has two main halls, the prayer hall and the *langar*. Other rooms include a library, a classroom for Panjabi and music lessons, an office for committee meetings, and sometimes rooms for visitors to stay overnight. Alcohol and tobacco are not permitted in the *gurdwara*.

Putting up the Nishan Sahib *outside a new* gurdwara

Many *gurdwaras* in India were built in places where special events in the lives of the gurus had taken place. These are described as the historic *gurdwaras*.

The most famous one, known throughout the world, is the Golden Temple. Its foundation stone was laid by a Muslim, Mian Mir, in 1588.

Probably the second most important historic *gurdwara* is the Akal Takhat, built in 1609 by the sixth guru, Guru Hargobind, in the Golden Temple complex. Meetings of the Sikh *Panth* (community) are held here to decide on major issues affecting Sikhs.

THE GRANTHI

Any man or woman may lead the service or read from the Guru Granth Sahib. However, it is normal practice for a *gurdwara* to employ and pay a learned and respected member of the community as its *granthi* (reader). The *granthi* generally leads services, reads from the Guru Granth Sahib, and performs all ceremonies. In a small *gurdwara*, he or she may act as caretaker as well.

Sikhs and anyone else who wants to worship God can come to a service at the *gurdwara* and eat in the *langar*. Prayers are said in the *gurdwara* every morning and evening. There is no fixed holy day of the week for Sikh worship. However, in the West, the majority of Sikhs attend services on either Saturdays or Sundays, because weekends are more convenient for most people.

The prayer hall

The focal point of every prayer hall is the Guru Granth Sahib, installed on its platform beneath a canopy. As a mark of respect for the Guru Granth Sahib, people must take off their shoes and cover their heads when they enter the hall. Those coming to worship pay their respects to the Guru Granth Sahib by bowing and touching the ground with their foreheads before they sit down. Generally they make token offerings of cash or food for the *langar*. Usually men and women sit separately, which is an Indian custom, but there are no strict religious rules about this.

Worship consists of *kirtan*, the singing of *shabads* from the Guru Granth Sahib accompanied by music on *tabla* (drums) and harmoniums (reed organs), and

This young boy is bowing before the Guru Granth Sahib before going to sit with the congregation

readings from the Guru Granth Sahib or a related religious text. Usually the congregation sits and listens to the *ragees* singing *kirtan*. Then everyone sings "Anand Sahib," the hymns composed by Guru Amar Das, the third guru. After that, the congregation stands up, with hands folded, and listens to the common prayer called the *ardas*. In this prayer, Sikhs first remember God, the gurus, and the Sikh martyrs, and then ask for God's blessings on all of humanity.

Ardas being said in the gurdwara

After the prayer, the whole congregation sits down and the *hukam* is read. The reader opens the Guru Granth Sahib at random and reads out a *shabad*. This is regarded as the guru's guidance for the day.

At the end of every service, *krah prashad* (the holy sweet) is distributed to everyone as a sign of the guru's blessings and to show that everyone is equal. *Krah prashad* is a sweet made from flour, sugar, water, and butter. The service is usually followed by sharing a meal in the *langar*.

A Sikh gathering for a service is called *diwan*. Sometimes political and social issues affecting the community are also discussed at the gathering.

Distributing krah prashad *at the end of the service*

A GURDWARA *IN MAKINDU, KENYA*

"The morning service in the *gurdwara* at Makindu starts at 7:00 a.m. and ends at 9:00 a.m. There is nothing unusual about this. What is out of the ordinary is the situation of the *gurdwara* and the makeup of the congregation.

"This beautiful *gurdwara* is in a small village on the main road between Nairobi and Mombasa. It was originally built in 1905 by Sikhs who had been brought from India to Africa by the British. Their job was to clear the jungle and construct a railroad line connecting Kenya's capital, Nairobi, to the east coast. In the jungle, these Sikhs had to fight both disease and wild animals—especially lions—and many of them lost their lives. It was in these conditions that they built a small *gurdwara* at Makindu.

"Now the *gurdwara* has been extended into a magnificent building surrounded by halls, rooms, and apartments, where up to two hundred people can eat and sleep for free. On many occasions, more than three thousand people are fed in a single day. On the day I visited, about two hundred visitors of all faiths, colors, and nationalities sat in the *langar* after the service and ate a breakfast of *dal* (curried lentils), *parathas* (bread), yogurt, and *matar paneer* (peas and cheese). There were white and Asian people of different religious backgrounds from England, a Muslim family from Canada, a group of Asian Hindus, five white young people from the United States, and a couple from Germany who were staying the night. All the costs of running the *gurdwara* are covered by donations from Sikhs and others.

"Sikhs have bought the land across the road from the *gurdwara* in order to establish an eye hospital, which is much needed in the area."
(Rema Kaur, London, England)

The langar

The *langar* is the common kitchen or dining hall of a *gurdwara*, but the word *langar* is also used for the free food that is served there. All people who attend a service at the *gurdwara* are expected to stay afterward to sit and eat together. This is a reminder that people of all races, classes, and faiths belong to the same family of humans and therefore should be treated equally. During the Mogul empire, even the emperor Akbar sat on the ground and shared the same *langar* as everyone else before he could see the guru.

The *langar* is run by donations and voluntary labor. Volunteers from the community make and distribute the food. Most families take turns cooking and serving it, and they consider this an honor.

The food served, which is also known sometimes as *guru ka langar*, usually consists of *dal* (lentils), a vegetable curry, *raita* (yogurt), rice, and chapattis. The food is always vegetarian so that everyone present is able to eat.

SEWA

Sewa means serving others, which is one of the main principles of Sikhism. Sikhs are taught to give their time, money, and skills to help others and to take pleasure in doing this, no matter how humble the job may be. Helping in the *langar* is one example of *sewa*.

Eating langar *after a service*

Learning Panjabi

Panth

The community of Sikhs who go to a *gurdwara* is called *Panth*. All men and women are equal members in it and may take part in discussing issues concerning Sikhs and deciding on what actions need to be taken.

Sikhs believe that the community is an important influence in forming the character of its members. A community therefore tries to give its children a basic knowledge and understanding of Sikhism. Most Sikh *gurdwaras* organize Panjabi and music classes, in which children and young people can learn to read and sing *shabads* from the Guru Granth Sahib and other scriptures written in Panjabi. Many Sikh organizations hold seminars, conferences, lectures, and weekend or week-long camps where lessons are given about the Sikh way of life.

In the West, Sikhs face some prejudice at school and when looking for jobs. For this reason, young Sikhs need a great deal of support from their families and the community to help them practice their religion without losing self-esteem.

Sikh children looking at Panjabi and Sikh history books

PRIZEWINNERS

Chetna Kaur Brar, age twelve, took part in a competition for young people organized by the Sikh International Hemkunt Education Council. Competitors in four age groups (7–11, 11–15, 15–18, and 18–25) had to answer questions on Sikh history. First there were competitions in eight different zones, two in each of Kenya, the United States, Canada, and Great Britain. The winners of each zonal competition, from each of the four age groups, went on to the final international competition. Chetna was the winner in one of the British zones, so she traveled to Nairobi, Kenya, where the finals were being held.

She was then competing with seven others, from different countries. First, second, and third medals would be awarded. All the participants had prepared for the questions they had to answer by studying books on Sikh history, which the Education Council had prescribed. When the results were announced Chetna found that she had come in second and won a gold medal, a certificate, and an ornamental brass clock. There was disappointment and jubilation among the participants. Chetna was delighted to have come in second, as in the previous two competitions held in Canada and in the United States she had not reached any of the first three positions.

Competitors also had an opportunity to enjoy some outings from Nairobi.

6

A SIKH LIFETIME

Sikhs have ceremonies to mark important events in their personal and family lives, such as the naming of a child, the time when a boy starts to wear a turban, marriage, and death. There is also a specifically religious ceremony called *Amrit Chhakna* by which a person is initiated as a Sikh.

The idea behind the ceremonies is to seek God's blessings and to renew one's spirit of devotion and service. All ceremonies are held in the presence of the Guru Granth Sahib and follow the form of a normal service of worship, including the singing of *shabads* suitable for the occasion and reading of the *ardas* and the *hukam*. *Krah prashad* is distributed and *langar* is provided for all the guests.

The naming ceremony

A family welcomes the birth of a baby boy or girl as a gift from God and celebrates this at the naming ceremony. When the mother is well enough, the family either goes to the *gurdwara* for the celebration or arranges for it to take place at home. In either case, the ceremony is performed in the presence of the Guru Granth Sahib. Sometimes a continuous reading of the whole Guru Granth Sahib is completed, to mark the occasion.

This family has just chosen the baby's name using the first letter of the hukam.

NAMING SIMRAN SINGH

When Mandeep's son was seven days old, she and her husband took him to her parents' home for his naming ceremony. It was to be a small family occasion. The baby's grandparents were just finishing a reading of the complete Guru Granth Sahib, so the service started with the reading of its last three pages. After singing *shabads*, the *ardas* was said. Then the *hukam* was read, which was, "O Lord, I seek only your protection." (GGS, p. 714). The first letter of this *shabad* in Panjabi is *s*. The baby's name was therefore to begin with that letter. After many suggestions, the family decided to name him Simran Singh.

During the service, *shabads* of thanksgiving are read and sung. They include one that Guru Arjan Dev, the fifth guru, composed on the birth of his son, Hargobind, who became the sixth guru:

> The True Lord has sent the child. The long lived child has been born by good fortune.
> The Sikhs sing God's praises in their joy.
>
> (GGS, p. 396)

The usual service takes place and, at the end, when the Guru Granth Sahib is opened at random for the *hukam*, the family listens for the first letter of the first word of the *shabad* that is read and chooses a name for the child that begins with that letter. As soon as they have decided on the name, they announce it to the congregation. Girls' named are followed by *kaur* (princess) and boys' names by *singh* (lion), as instructed by Guru Gobind Singh, the tenth guru (see page 12). Most Sikh names can be used for both boys and girls. For example, a girl might be named Mandeep Kaur and a boy Mandeep Singh. Sometimes a family name is added, which could be the name of the area from which the family originally came.

The marriage ceremony

The Sikh marriage ceremony is called *Anand Karaj*, which means the ceremony of joy. Marriage in Sikhism is considered not just a social or civil contract but also a spiritual union. The love between wife and husband is compared with the love and longing of the human soul for God.

The bride and groom sit in front of the Guru Granth Sahib. The person who officiates at the ceremony (who may be a *granthi*, but can be any Sikh man or woman) asks them and their parents to stand while the *ardas* is said. This is both to seek the gurus' blessings and to show the parents' and the congregation's approval of the marriage. Then the officiator explains the significance of Sikh marriage, in which husband and wife are equal partners. The couple is reminded of their duties to each other and their obligations to society at large.

Walking around the Guru Granth Sahib. This bride and groom are wearing traditional Punjabi clothes.

After this short lecture, the bride and groom are asked to show their assent to the marriage by bowing before the Guru Granth Sahib. The bride's father places one end of a *pala* (scarf) in the groom's hand and the other in the bride's. The *pala* symbolizes the soft but strong bond between husband and wife, and the couple holds on to it throughout the rest of the ceremony.

The Guru Granth Sahib is opened and the marriage *shabad*, "Lavan," is read. The *granthi* reads the first verse, and then it is sung by the *ragees*. The couple rises, still holding the ends of the *pala*. They walk slowly around the Guru Granth Sahib, with the groom leading. On reaching their starting position, they bow to the Guru Granth Sahib and sit down to hear the second verse being read. As before, the *ragees* then sing the verse and the couple walks around the Guru Granth Sahib. This is repeated for the remaining two verses, after which the service continues as usual.

The death ceremony

When a family member dies, the Guru Granth Sahib reminds Sikhs that:

> The dawn of a new day is the message of a sunset.
> Earth is not the permanent home.   (GGS, p. 793)

Sikhs are told to avoid shows of grief, to find comfort in reading the Guru Granth Sahib, and to accept God's will.

In India the weather is hot and arrangements for the refrigeration of bodies are not common. Therefore bodies are cremated within a day or so of death. In the West, there is usually a longer time between death and cremation, depending on the availability of the crematorium.

On the day of the cremation, the body is washed and dressed in the five ks and brought home for family and friends to pay their last respects. Then it is taken to the crematorium in a procession or motorcade.

LAVAN

"Lavan" is a hymn in four verses, written by Guru Ram Das. *Lavan* means "circling."

The first verse stresses the importance of married life for serving God and truth. It discards the idea that a person who dedicates his life to God should remain single.

The second compares the joy of finding a marriage partner with the joy of the soul when God is present in a person's life.

The third says that, just as the couple's love for one another makes everything else seem unimportant, so for the soul that has found God, all other things are unimportant by comparison.

The fourth says that the marriage is now complete, in the same way as the soul reaches perfect union with God.

DEATH AND REBIRTH

Sikhs believe that death is not the end. The person's soul is born again. This is called the transmigration of souls.

Human birth is an opportunity to find and be united with God. If a person misses this opportunity, then he or she has to go into the cycle of birth and death again.

Sikhs are taught that each human being has free will to choose to be good or bad. The family into which a person is born is decided according to karma (good or bad actions in the previous life). By leading a good life and serving the needy, one can improve and come closer to God.

Four of the five ks: undergarment, comb, bangle, and sword.

At the crematorium, the *kirtan sohila* (*shabads* for evening prayers) are recited and *ardas* is said to ask for peace for the departed soul. The ashes are usually thrown into a river or the sea.

Finally there is a ceremony called *Bhog* (the completion of life's journey). The family has probably marked the occasion of the person's death with a complete reading of the Guru Granth Sahib, performed at intervals, at home or at the *gurdwara*. This is called the *Sehaj Path*. The last five pages are read at the *Bhog* ceremony, and then the usual service takes place.

The amrit *ceremony*

The *amrit* ceremony is the ceremony of initiation into the *Khalsa Panth* (the Sikh community). Any man or woman who is prepared to accept the rules governing the Sikh community has the right to receive *amrit*. Sometimes *amrit* is called *khande ka pahul*, which is nectar prepared by dissolving sugar crystals in water by stirring them with a double-edged sword. The double-edged sword reminds Sikhs that the members of the Khalsa should be "saint-soldiers"—women and men who are prepared to use arms to defend the weak and oppressed without feeling bitterness toward their enemies. There is no minimum age for taking *amrit*, but young people are advised to take *amrit* when they understand the meaning of the vows they have to take.

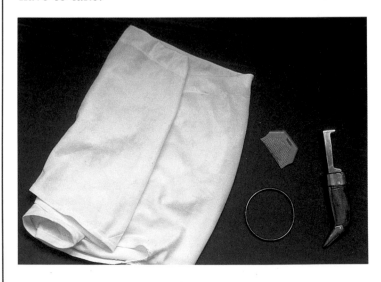

The khanda *symbol consists of a double-edged sword, for God's power as Creator, a circle for continuity, and two swords representing the spiritual and the political elements of the universe.*

Those taking *amrit* come to the ceremony wearing the five ks. It usually takes place in the *gurdwara* and always in the presence of the Guru Granth Sahib. Five people conduct the ceremony, representing the *Panj Piarey* (the five beloved ones) who became the first members of the *Khalsa* when it was established by Guru Gobind Singh, the tenth guru. Another Sikh is present to read the Guru Granth Sahib, but apart from that the *amrit* ceremony is not witnessed by anyone else.

At the start, one of the *Panj Piarey* explains the rules and obligations of being a Sikh. Those receiving *amrit* agree to accept these obligations, and then the *ardas* is said and a *shabad* is read from the Guru Granth Sahib opened at random. Clean water and sugar crystals are put in a steel bowl. The Panj Piarey stir the water with a double-edged sword while reciting five prayers. After the prayers, those taking *amrit* receive it in cupped hands and drink it five times. The *amrit* is also sprinkled five times on their eyes and hair. The ceremony ends with the usual service.

The duties of a Sikh may be summarized as follows:

- to recite the five sacred prayers daily

- to give up all caste and class differences

- never to do the four forbidden acts, which are: to cut one's hair; to use tobacco, alcohol or other harmful drugs; to commit adultery; and to eat *halal* meat (that is, meat killed according to Muslim religious practice). Sikhs eat only *jhatka* meat, which is from animals killed with a single blow.

7

The times of Sikh festivals are calculated according to the lunar calendar, which is used in India.

The main Sikh festivals described in this chapter fall in the following months on the international calendar:

Baisakhi – April

Diwali –
October/November

**Birthday of Guru
Nanak** –
October/November

**Birthday of Guru
Gobind Singh** –
December/January

**Martyrdom of Guru
Tegh Bahadur** –
November/December

**Martyrdom of Guru
Arjan Dev** – June

FESTIVALS

Festivals, which are also called *Gurpurabs* (gurus' days), give Sikhs a chance to rededicate themselves to their faith. On these occasions, Sikhs celebrate important events connected with the gurus' lives by saying prayers in their *gurdwaras* and sometimes by taking part in processions.

Panj Piarey *lead the procession to celebrate* Baisakhi.

Sikhs give money and other offerings to charities and participate in *sewa*, providing free services to people in need. On *Gurpurabs* some Sikh doctors give free blood tests, dentists offer free dental check-ups, and other Sikhs may cook and distribute food to the poor. In a *gurdwara* in the United States, Sikh doctors examined more than four hundred patients free of charge on one festival day, and free meals were also provided.

There are a large number of *Gurpurabs*. Only the main ones are described here. Even the anniversaries of the gurus' martyrdoms are positive celebrations, because the gurus' sacrifices remind Sikhs of their own duties to society.

All the festivals are celebrated with *Akhand Path*, the continuous reading of the Guru Granth Sahib, which is completed on the morning of the festival day. This is followed by the singing of *shabads*, talks about the importance and meaning of the festival, and then the usual Sikh service. In India, people usually observe the festivals by taking the Guru Granth Sahib in a procession through the city or village. The Guru Granth Sahib is carried on a float covered with flowers, and *Panj Piarey* head the procession.

Baisakhi

Baisakhi is an Indian New Year festival, which usually falls in April in the Western, international calendar. It was on the occasion of this festival that Guru Gobind Singh, the tenth guru, introduced and conducted the first *amrit* ceremony.

A new flag is ready to be flown

A tradition on this day is to renew the *Nishan Sahib*, the Sikh flag, which flies from each *gurdwara*. A service led by five Sikhs representing the *Panj Piarey* is held outside. The flag post is taken down and the *chola*, the flag cloth, is removed. The flag post is washed, covered with a new *chola*, and re-hoisted. The ceremony ends with saying the *ardas*.

At most *gurdwaras* the *amrit* ceremony is performed on this day. Also, there are competitions in many subjects, such as sports, martial arts, music, poetry, essay writing, and public speaking.

Illuminations at the Golden Temple

Diwali

Diwali means "the festival of lights." On *Diwali* day Sikhs celebrate the arrival in Amritsar of Guru Hargobind, the sixth guru, after he had been released from prison. The Mogul emperor Jehangir had imprisoned the guru on the charge of raising an army and committing treason against him. When the case was examined, the charge was found to be baseless and the guru was released. In the same prison the guru had met 52 Hindu princes, or rajas, who were also innocent. When he was released, he refused to accept his liberty unless the rajas were also set free. He was told that as many princes as could pass through the narrow passage of the jail and out into the outside world while holding onto his cloak, would be freed. The guru asked for a cloak with 52 tassels; by each holding on to one of these, all the rajas managed to get their freedom.

To celebrate the story, Sikhs illuminate the entire Golden Temple complex, and there are wonderful displays of fireworks. The treasures and weapons used by the gurus are also exhibited at this festival time.

Candles lit for Diwali

The birthdays of Guru Nanak and Guru Gobind Singh

Sikhs celebrate with great spirit the birthdays of the founder of the religion and of the last guru in human form. In Punjab, *gurdwaras*, shops, offices, and houses are lit with candles. Children are given new clothes and have a day off from school to join in the festival processions.

In these procession, the Guru Granth Sahib is installed on a beautifully decorated *palki* (platform). *Panj Piarey* lead the procession, followed by Sikhs singing *shabads*, schoolchildren joining in with their music bands, and young people giving displays of martial arts.

A float is being prepared to carry the Guru Granth Sahib in a procession to celebrate Guru Nanak's birthday

Special celebrations are held at Nanakana Sahib, the birthplace of Guru Nanak, which is now in Pakistan.

The martyrdom of Guru Tegh Bahadur

At this festival, Sikhs remember Guru Tegh Bahadur, the ninth guru, who sacrificed his life for the religious freedom of all people. Large numbers of Sikhs gather in the Gurdwara Sis Ganj in Delhi, where the guru was beheaded by the orders of the Mogul emperor Aurangzeb.

THE MARTYRDOM OF GURU ARJAN DEV

It is June, the hottest month of the year in Punjab. Everywhere, especially in Amritsar, roadside stalls have been set up from which Sikhs are serving passersby with free cool, refreshing drinks. There are stalls offering all sorts of sodas and other sweet drinks.

These Sikhs are remembering the thirst of their fifth guru, Guru Arjan Dev, who was tortured to death by having hot sand poured onto his near-naked body in the heat of an Indian June in 1606. This guru stood for tolerance and the right of all people to worship as they choose. He taught that no one religion is the only true religion. For saying this, he was martyred and his followers were persecuted.

It is in keeping with the guru's teachings on tolerance that Sikhs commemorate the anniversary of his sufferings by attending to the thirst of all people, whatever their race and belief.

Glossary

To show how words are pronounced, some letters have been underlined in the words in this Glossary.

chh — there is no equivalent sound in English. It sounds like the *ch* in *church*, but with the *h* held a little longer.
u — sounds like *u* in *bull*
a — sounds like *a* in *am*
a̲ — sounds like *a* in *car*
i — sounds like *i* in *sit*
i̲ — sounds like *ee* in *meet*

amrit — Literally, nectar. This is made by stirring sugar crystals into water with a double-edged sword while certain passages from the scriptures are read.

Amrit Chhakna̲ — The Sikh rite of initiation into the *Khalsa*.

arda̲s — A formal prayer offered at most religious services and occasions.

chandni̲ — A canopy placed over the Guru Granth Sahib, used as a mark of respect.

chouri̲ — A fan made of yak hair or nylon, which is waved over the Guru Granth Sahib to show respect for the scriptures.

diwan — A congregational gathering for worship.

granthi̲ — Reader of the Guru Granth Sahib, who officiates at ceremonies and may also act as a caretaker of the *gurdwara*.

gurdwara — Sikh place of worship.

Gurmukhi — "From the Guru's mouth"; name given to the script in which the scriptures and the Panjabi language are written.

hukam — Random reading taken for guidance from the Guru Granth Sahib.

kachh — Traditional underwear/shorts; one of the five *k*s worn by both male and female Sikhs.

kanga̲ — Comb worn in the hair; one of the five *k*s.

kara̲ — Steel bangle; one of the five *k*s worn by both male and female Sikhs.

ka̲ur — Literally, princess; a name given to every Sikh female. The name was given by Guru Gobind Singh to elevate the position of women.

kes — Uncut hair; one of the five *k*s.

Khalsa — The community of the pure; the Sikh community.

Kirat Karni — Earning one's livelihood by one's own efforts.

kirpan — Sword; one of the five *k*s. (The term *dagger* should be avoided.)

kirtan — Devotional singing of compositions from the Guru Granth Sahib, the Dasam Granth, and the Bhai Gurdas.

kra̲h pra̲sha̲d — A food made of flour, sugar, butter, or ghee (purified butter) in equal proportions. It is shared at the end of Sikh gatherings to symbolize equality.

langar — Gurus' kitchen; the *gurdwara* dining hall and the food served in it.

*la*v*an*	The part of a marriage ceremony where the couple walk around the Guru Granth Sahib. Also, the name of the four verses from the Guru Granth Sahib that are said at the ceremony.
Nam Japna	Meditation on God's name, using passages from scripture.
Nishan Sahib	Sikh flag flown at gurdwaras and at other Sikh buildings. The flag is saffron-colored, triangular, and has the khanda symbol on it.
palki	The structure in which the Guru Granth Sahib is ceremonially installed.
Panj Piarey	The five beloved ones; the first five men initiated into the *Khalsa*.
Panth	The Sikh community.
patka	A head-covering used by boys before they start wearing turbans.
ragee	Sikh musician who leads and sings compositions from the Guru Granth Sahib.
romallas	Cloths used as coverings for the Guru Granth Sahib.
sangat	Congregation or assembly of Sikhs.
sewa	Service, an essential part of the life of every Sikh.
shabad	Hymn from the Guru Granth Sahib.
singh	Literally, lion. A name used by all Sikh males.
Vand Chhakna	Sharing one's time, talents, and earnings with the less fortunate.

Book List

Ashton, Stephen. *The British in India*. North Pomfret, VT: Trafalgar Square, 1988.

Bawa, Ujagar S. *Sikhism: A Short Expose*. Gaithersburg, MD: Washington Sikh Center, 1988.

Bennett, Olivia. *Sikh Wedding*. North Pomfret, VT: Trafalgar Square, 1991.

Cumming, David. *India*. Economically Developing Countries. New York: Thomson Learning, 1995.

Dhanjal, Beryl. *Amritsar*. Holy Cities. New York: Dillon Press, 1994.

Kapoor. *Sikh Festivals*. Vero Beach, FL: Rourke Corp., 1989.

Morris, Scott E., ed. *Religions of the World*. Using and Understanding Maps. New York: Chelsea House, 1993.

Singh, Nikkyh-Guninder. *Sikhism*. New York: Facts on File, 1992.

Warner, Rachel. *Indian Migrations*. Migrations. New York: Thomson Learning, 1995.

Note on Dates

Each religion has its own system for counting the years of its history. The starting point may be related to the birth or death of a special person or an important event. In everyday life, today, when different communities have dealings with each other, they need to use the same counting system for setting dates in the future and writing accounts of the past. The Western system is now used throughout the world. It is based on Christian beliefs about Jesus: A.D. (*Anno Domini* = in the year of our Lord) and B.C. (Before Christ). Members of the various world faiths use the common Western system, but, instead of A.D. and B.C., they say and write C.E. (in the Common Era) and B.C.E. (before the Common Era).

Index